Our Baby has

Sixty-Five Roses

Written by Eilís Moroney   Illustrated by Ruth Cahill

My Mummy had a baby in her tummy.
Everyone was so excited!!

I wanted Mummy to have **a girl** and
Baxter the dog wanted Mummy to have **a boy**.

Mummy's tummy grew and grew.
Soon it was time for her to go to the hospital
to have the baby.

I couldn't wait to meet my
new brother or sister!

I stayed with Granny and Grandad and
Daddy drove Mummy to the hospital.

That evening I was **SO excited** that I could barely sleep!!

The next morning, we got a phone call from Daddy.

I had a new **baby sister!**

Mummy had given birth to a girl!!

Later that day, I visited my baby sister in the hospital.

I was so excited to **meet my sister** for the first time.

Mummy and the baby came home a day or two later.

My little sister was hungry all of the time!!

And she did a lot
of dirty nappies too.

After a while, my little sister's tummy
was starting to get a bit sore.
Her tummy aches made her cry!

Then Mummy got a phone call from the hospital.

A nurse wanted to meet my baby sister.

She thought that my baby sister
might have **sixty-five roses**.

Sixty-five
roses?

Mummy and Daddy were very worried
when they got this phone call.
Granny and Grandad
were worried too.

I wondered,
'Why are they worrying about sixty-five roses?
Roses are beautiful.'

Mummy and Daddy brought
my sister to the hospital.
The nurse was right!

My little sister **did** have sixty-five roses.

When Mummy and Daddy came home from the hospital
they brought some medicine with them.

This will make
her tummy better'
Daddy told me.

'Your little sister has Cystic Fibrosis', explained Dad.

'It means that she will sometimes get more coughs and colds than other people. But we will mind her and love her and help keep any nasty germs away.'

'I don't want her to have coughs and colds Dad.
I just want her to have sixty-five beautiful roses'.

'Well, let's do that then',
said Dad.

ROSE GARDEN

HOW TO GROW A GARDEN OF ROSES

SEEDS

My little sister gobbles her apple purée
and enzymes before she drinks her milk.

She **loves** them!

And now her tummy is all better!

Mummy and Daddy put some salt in her milk too and they make
sure that she gets all of the vitamins that she needs.

We all make sure that we wash our
hands before holding my little sister.

Everyday, my Daddy bounces my sister
on an exercise ball for 15 minutes.

She loves it!!

Daddy says that the bouncing will help keep
her lungs strong and healthy.

The bouncing is SO much fun......
and I love when Daddy bounces me too!

Sometimes, Mummy brings me to the hospital for my baby sister's appointments.

The doctors and nurses are so nice and friendly.
They really love looking after my sister!

When my baby sister gets a cough or a cold,
the nurses and doctors mind her.

They **help protect** her sixty-five roses.

My little sister has Cystic Fibrosis. But she has lots of other things too...

Courage
Contentment
Humour
Ambition
Love
Giggles
Mischief
Curiosity
Excitement
Resilience
Happiness
Determination
Personality
Joy
Tickles
Value
Feelings

My sister is my sister. And I love her.

To CF Ireland for their brilliant support in publishing this book.

CF House, 24 Lower Rathmines Road, Dublin 6.   Web: www.cfireland.ie   Email: info@cfireland.ie   Tel: +353 (0)1 496 2433